VOICES

STUDY GUIDE

VOICES

The Power, Pain, & Purpose of Voices

SAM CHAND

STUDY GUIDE

AVAIL

CONTENTS

VOICES

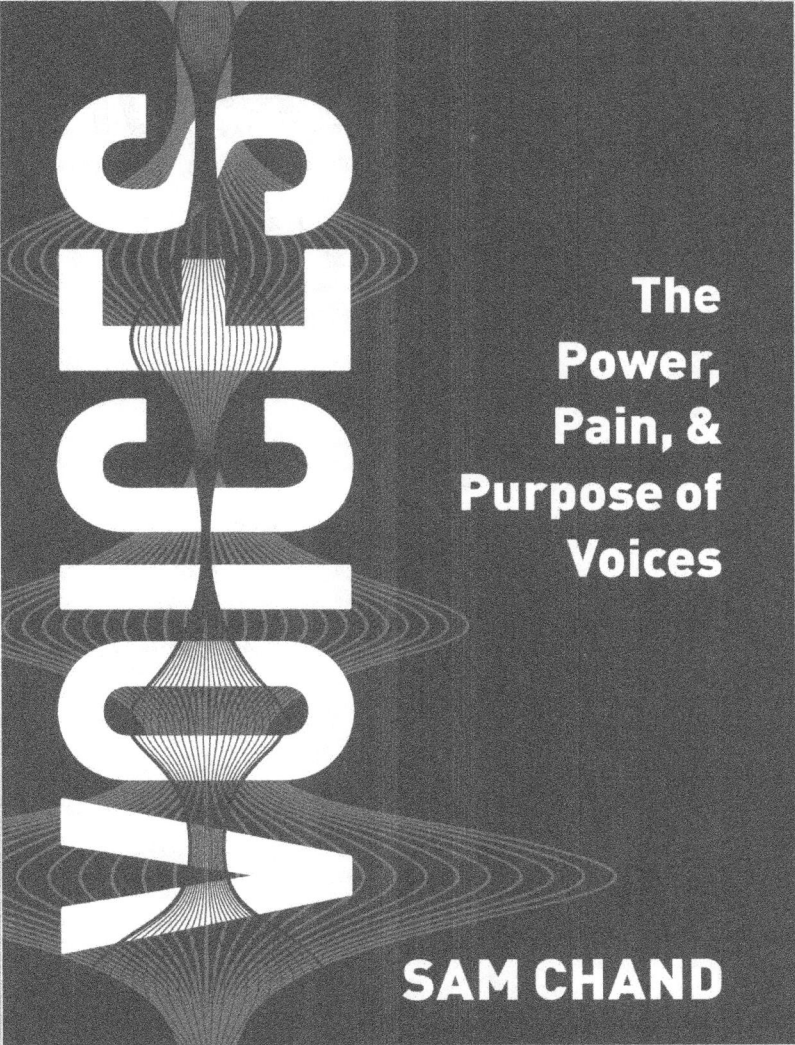

The Power, Pain, & Purpose of Voices

SAM CHAND

VOICES WE'VE HEARD

Whose voice is resident in your head?

READING TIME

As you read Chapter 1: "Voices We've Heard" in *Voices*, reflect on, and respond to the text by answering the following questions.

REFLECT AND TAKE ACTION:

What are some of the most affirming voices you've heard throughout your life?

_____

_____

_____

_____

_____

_____

_____

_____

_____

Take yourself back to the above. What did you feel when those words were spoken? What difference did these people make when they spoke to you this way?

_____

_____

_____

_____

_____

_____

_____

_____

As you read this chapter, you probably had a flashback or two of harsh, uncaring things people have said to you. What were the messages, both verbal and non-verbal? What did you feel when you heard these messages? What impact did they have on you—short-term and long-term?

_____

_____

_____

_____

_____

_____

_____

What are some of the strangest and funniest things people have said to you?

_____

_____

_____

_____

_____

_____

_____

How do you balance the influence of personal and professional voices when making leadership decisions?

_____

_____

_____

_____

_____

What techniques can you implement to ensure your leadership positively impacts team culture and performance?

_____

_____

_____

_____

_____

_____

_____

How can you foster an environment that encourages adaptive leadership and continuous improvement within your team?

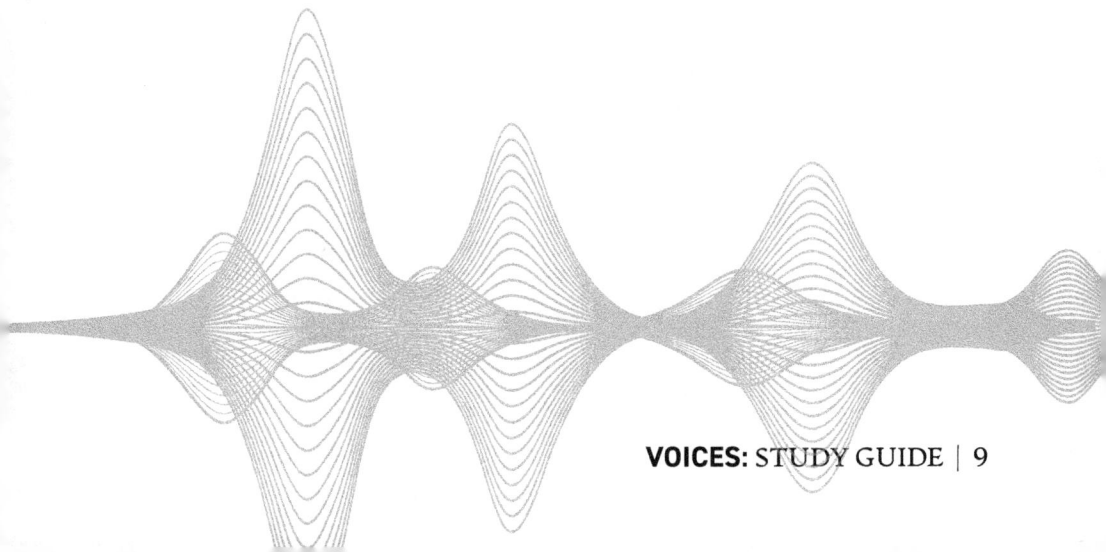

_____

_____

_____

_____

_____

_____

_____

VOICES WE'VE IGNORED

Isn't it ironic that the voices we long to hear are often the ones we ignore?

READING TIME

As you read
Chapter 2:
"Voices We've
Ignored"
in *Voices*,
reflect on,
and respond
to the text by
answering
the following
questions.

REFLECT AND TAKE ACTION:

Can you relate to Pastor Robert in
the opening story of this chapter? If
so, how?

_____

_____

_____

_____

_____

_____

_____

What are some voices you allow to be
too loud and too frequent?

_____

_____

_____

_____

_____

_____

What are some important voices
you've ignored?

_____

_____

_____

_____

_____

Describe what it will take to replace your filter.

_____

_____

_____

_____

_____

_____

How can you effectively manage and respond to negative feedback while maintaining your confidence and focus?

_____

_____

_____

_____

_____

_____

What practical steps can you take to ensure positive and constructive voices are given more weight in your decision-making process?

_____

_____

_____

_____

_____

_____

How can you balance the need for constructive criticism with the necessity of receiving affirmations from trusted individuals?

_____

_____

_____

_____

_____

_____

What steps can you take to cultivate a supportive network that provides both honest feedback and affirmations to enhance your leadership?

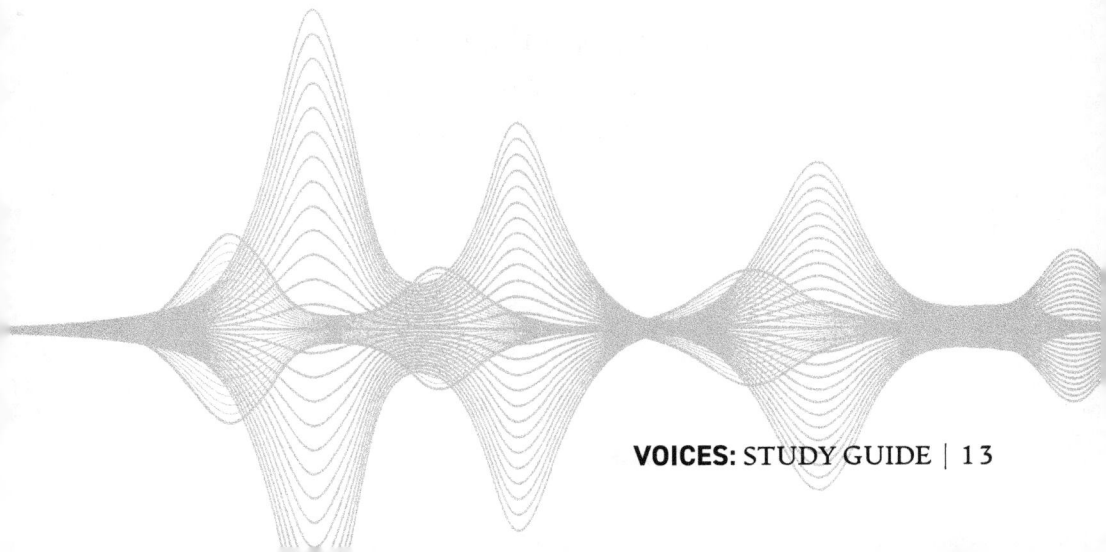

_____

_____

_____

_____

_____

_____

VOICES OF TOXIC MESSAGES

The problem is that we give toxic messages far too much space in our heads.

READING TIME

As you read Chapter 3: "Voices of Toxic Messages" in *Voices*, reflect on, and respond to the text by answering the following questions.

REFLECT AND TAKE ACTION:

What's the language of your inner critic (we all have one)? Why do these messages seem so right and normal?

_____

_____

_____

_____

_____

_____

_____

_____

_____

_____

How does feeling misunderstood affect you? What's your go-to remedy (helpful or unhelpful)?

_____

_____

_____

_____

_____

_____

_____

_____

_____

_____

Do you agree or disagree that change has become the new normal, which makes many of us feel out of control?

_____

_____

_____

_____

_____

_____

_____

When are comparison and competition healthy? When are they toxic?

_____

_____

_____

_____

_____

_____

_____

_____

What are some consequences of "when-then" thinking?

_____

_____

_____

_____

_____

_____

_____

_____

Can you identify a past experience that significantly influenced your self-esteem or self-worth, and how does it impact your current actions and decisions?

_____

_____

_____

_____

_____

_____

What strategies can you employ to recognize and challenge toxic thoughts, and how can positive affirmations or scripture help in this process?

_____

_____

_____

_____

_____

_____

Reflect on a time when comparison motivated you positively and another when it led to negative feelings; what factors made the difference?

_____

_____

_____

_____

_____

_____

VOICES WE LONG TO HEAR

No matter how much success we've enjoyed, no matter how many difficulties we've overcome, we still need to hear voices that validate our value.

READING TIME

As you read Chapter 4: "Voices We Long to Hear" in *Voices*, reflect on, and respond to the text by answering the following questions.

REFLECT AND TAKE ACTION:

Does it amaze you that every person Oprah has interviewed asked if they did okay? Why?

_____

_____

_____

_____

_____

_____

_____

_____

_____

_____

What voice do you need to hear—and not need to hear—when you're angry?

_____

_____

_____

_____

_____

_____

_____

_____

_____

_____

When experiencing anger, how does the voice of validation differ from the voice of dismissal? How does each affect your ability to manage and express your emotions constructively?

_____

_____

_____

_____

_____

_____

What voice do you need to hear—and not need to hear—when you're hurt and afraid?

_____

_____

_____

_____

_____

_____

_____

In moments of hurt and fear, what role does genuine empathy play in providing validation and support? How does this differ from attempts to offer solutions or minimize the significance of one's feelings?

_____

_____

_____

_____

_____

_____

What voice do you need to hear—and not need to hear—when you're confused?

_____

_____

_____

_____

_____

_____

When facing confusion, how does validation of your feelings and perceptions help clarify your thoughts and guide your decision-making process? How can others effectively provide this validation?

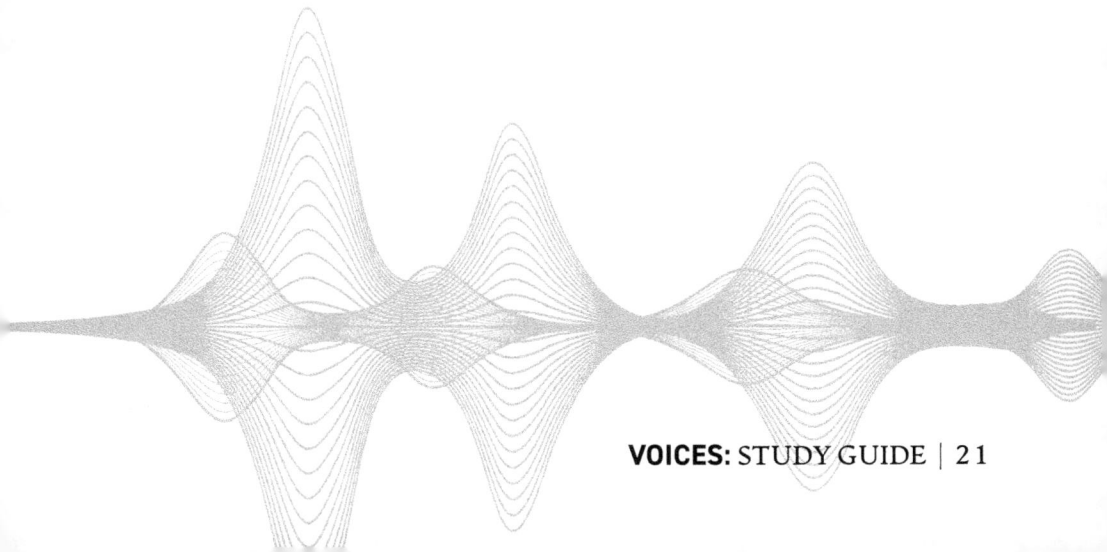

_____

_____

_____

_____

_____

_____

What voice do you need to hear—and not need to hear—when you're inspired?

_____

_____

_____

_____

_____

_____

_____

_____

_____

_____

Reflecting on times of inspiration and achievement, how does specific and genuine affirmation impact your motivation and confidence? How does this type of validation differ from generic praise?

_____

_____

_____

_____

_____

_____

_____

_____

_____

_____

_____

Think about the people you care about and consider the variety of emotional states discussed in the chapter, how can you tailor your communication to provide the right kind of validation and support to those around you?

_____

_____

_____

_____

_____

_____

_____

_____

_____

_____

_____

_____

_____

_____

MICRO-VOICES

Hear the voices. Pay attention to them. They might lead you to one of the cracks so you can address the problems before it becomes a disaster.

READING TIME

As you read
Chapter 5:
"Micro-
Voices" in
Voices, reflect
on, and
respond to
the text by
answering
the following
questions.

REFLECT AND TAKE ACTION:

Which two or three of the powerful voices do you hear most often or most acutely?

_____

_____

_____

_____

_____

_____

Where are the voices coming from? How do they affect you?

_____

_____

_____

_____

_____

_____

_____

How have you tried to manage them?

_____

_____

_____

_____

_____

_____

_____

Write an inspection plan. Who will you choose as the chief inspector? How will implementing the plan affect your well-being, your most important relationships, and your leadership?

_____

_____

_____

_____

_____

_____

Reflecting on the analogy of the Silver Bridge collapse, how do micro-stresses, communicated through micro-voices, gradually weaken an individual's resilience over time?

_____

_____

_____

_____

_____

_____

When facing criticism, how do individuals typically respond emotionally? How can the impact of critical voices be mitigated to maintain confidence and resilience?

_____

_____

_____

_____

_____

Considering the emotional rollercoaster experienced by leaders, how can they effectively manage dramatic ups and downs in their personal and professional lives?

_____

_____

_____

_____

_____

_____

In the face of demands for excellence, how can leaders maintain motivation and confidence while navigating challenges and potential confrontations with critics?

_____

_____

_____

_____

_____

How can leaders effectively prioritize tasks and manage their time to minimize stress and maintain productivity?

_____

_____

_____

_____

_____

COMPETING VOICES

We are in the world but not of the world—our job, every minute of every day, is to discern between the conflicting voices.

As you read
Chapter 6:
"Competing
Voices" in
Voices, reflect
on, and
respond to
the text by
answering
the following
questions.

REFLECT AND TAKE ACTION:

Which of the leaders in this chapter do
you identify with most closely? Why?

_____

_____

_____

_____

_____

_____

_____

_____

_____

_____

What were the conflicting voices the
person you identified in question 1
heard and spoke?

_____

_____

_____

_____

_____

_____

_____

_____

_____

What are the conflicting voices you hear and speak?

_____

_____

_____

_____

_____

_____

What are the conflicting voices on your team and in your church or organization today?

_____

_____

_____

_____

_____

_____

_____

Recall a time when you felt like the man in Aesop's story, torn between competing voices giving you conflicting advice. Describe the situation and how it made you feel.

_____

_____

_____

_____

_____

_____

How do you handle situations where the voices of those around you are criticizing your decisions or actions, similar to how Noah may have felt during the construction of the ark?

_____

_____

_____

_____

_____

_____

When faced with uncertainty, do you tend to lean towards taking risks like Joseph, or do you prefer a more cautious approach?

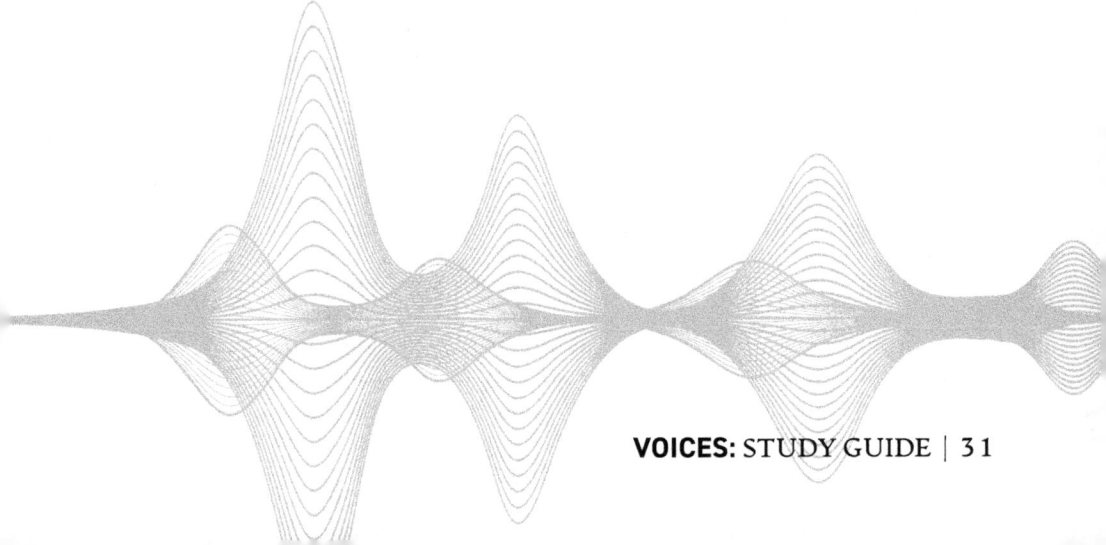

_____

_____

_____

_____

_____

_____

Have you ever been in a position where you felt torn between your own ambitions and God's calling, similar to Moses's struggle with his identity and purpose?

_____

_____

_____

_____

_____

_____

_____

_____

_____

_____

_____

How do you navigate through moments of self-doubt and uncertainty, particularly after experiencing success or achieving significant milestones, similar to Elijah's experience after the showdown on Mount Carmel?

_____

_____

_____

_____

_____

_____

_____

_____

_____

_____

_____

Can you recall a time when you had to discern between the voices of authority figures or influencers in your life and the voice of God, similar to Paul's transformation on the road to Damascus?

_____

_____

_____

_____

_____

_____

_____

_____

_____

_____

_____

_____

_____

_____

SCREENING THE VOICES

One of the most important tasks is separating the noise from what's truly meaningful.

READING TIME

As you read Chapter 7: "Screening the Voices" in *Voices*, reflect on, and respond to the text by answering the following questions.

REFLECT AND TAKE ACTION:

What are some of the most common ads you see? What's their surface message? What is their real promise?

_____

_____

_____

_____

_____

_____

Why is confirmation bias so attractive? What damage does it do?

_____

_____

_____

_____

_____

_____

What are the most important and effective ways you screen the voices that come into your life?

_____

_____

_____

_____

_____

_____

_____

How would you describe "positive affective presence"?
Who has that role in your life? How well are you being
that kind of leader?

_____

_____

_____

_____

_____

_____

What practical steps can we take to identify and
dismantle the negative influences that seek to undermine
our faith and well-being?

_____

_____

_____

_____

_____

_____

What strategies can individuals employ to effectively
separate the noise from the meaningful voices in their lives?

_____

_____

_____

_____

_____

_____

How does confirmation bias hinder our ability to engage with opposing viewpoints and build bridges with others, both personally and professionally?

_____

_____

_____

_____

_____

_____

Reflecting on the concept of "positive affective presence," who are the individuals in your life that embody this trait, and how can you cultivate it within yourself as a leader?

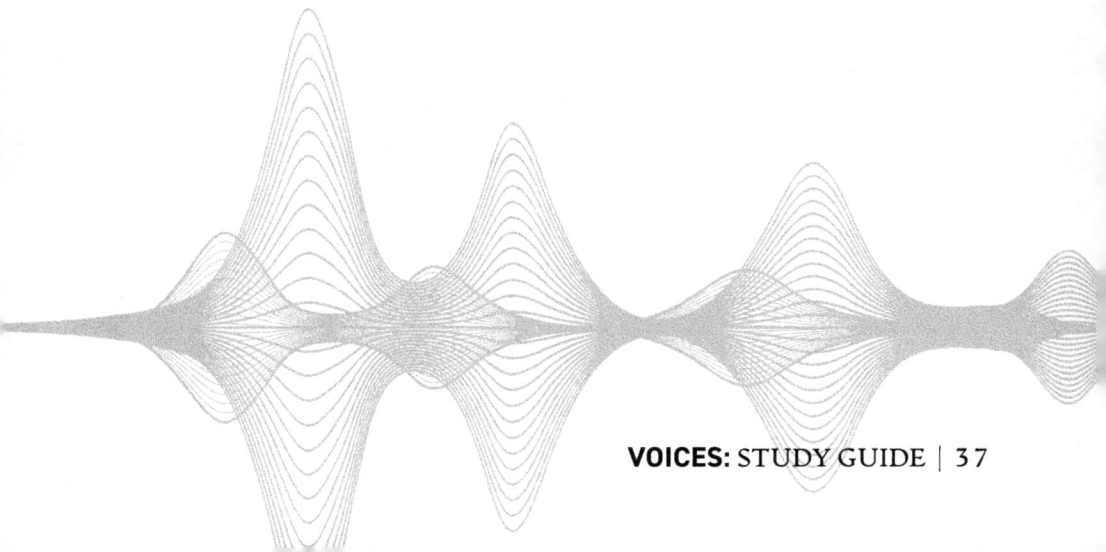

_____

_____

_____

_____

_____

_____

CHAPTER 8

QUESTIONING VOICES

Questions are important voices.
They make people think more deeply,
uncover hidden opportunities,
and shake up the system.

REFLECT AND TAKE ACTION:

Take some time to ask yourself the questions in the first part of this chapter.

What are two or three major applications of your above reflection?

_____

_____

_____

_____

_____

_____

When, where, and how often do you want to pose questions to your leaders?

_____

_____

_____

_____

_____

_____

What difference do you think doing the above will make?

_____

_____

_____

_____

_____

_____

Which of the questions about organizations are most important for you to ask at this point? Where do you expect pushback?

_____

_____

_____

_____

_____

_____

What are some ways to bring people (your team, top lay leaders, and the whole organization) along?

_____

_____

_____

_____

_____

_____

What strategies can you employ to amplify voices of encouragement and affirmation while minimizing the influence of self-doubt within yourself?

_____

_____

_____

_____

_____

_____

How can you ensure that organizational priorities remain focused amid the challenges of growth and change?

_____

_____

_____

_____

_____

_____

In times of stress, what steps can you take to cultivate a supportive environment and seek expert advice for navigating difficult circumstances?

_____

_____

_____

_____

_____

What are the key considerations for leaders when delegating responsibilities and structuring their teams to foster innovation and productivity?

_____

_____

_____

_____

_____

_____

TAILORING YOUR VOICE

It's crucial to tailor your voice of vision to meet the needs of the moment—and sometimes, those needs aren't evident yet.

READING TIME

As you read Chapter 9: "Tailoring Your Voice" in *Voices*, reflect on, and respond to the text by answering the following questions.

REFLECT AND TAKE ACTION:

As you look at the S-curve, where is your organization in the growth cycle?

_____

_____

_____

_____

_____

_____

What kind of resistance can you expect (from your own inertia and your leaders) if you share a new vision that propels the organization into a period of uncertainty and change?

_____

_____

_____

_____

_____

_____

Will the above be worth the hassle? Why or why not?

_____

_____

_____

_____

_____

_____

If you were a consultant, what questions would you ask yourself? How would you answer them?

_____

_____

_____

_____

_____

_____

_____

What steps do you need to take to future-proof your organization and yourself?

_____

_____

_____

_____

_____

_____

_____

How can you ensure that your leadership pipeline consistently produces competent new leaders to sustain growth?

_____

_____

_____

_____

_____

_____

_____

In what ways can you tailor your leadership voice to address the specific needs of your organization at its current phase?

_____

_____

_____

_____

_____

_____

What strategies can you implement to inject fresh energy and vision into your organization before it reaches a plateau?

_____

_____

_____

_____

_____

_____

How can you foster a culture of collaboration within your organization to drive lasting change effectively?

_____

_____

_____

_____

_____

_____

USE YOUR VOICE FOR GOOD

*What is your voice in the lives
of those around you?*

READING TIME

As you read Chapter 10: "Use Your Voice for Good" in *Voices*, reflect on, and respond to the text by answering the following questions.

REFLECT AND TAKE ACTION:

What are you doing well, and what can you improve as you use your voice to create a cohesive culture? What about celebrating creativity? What about blending boldness and humility?

_____

_____

_____

_____

_____

_____

_____

_____

Whose voices do you need to listen to more closely?

_____

_____

_____

_____

_____

Whose voices do you need to ignore or refute?

_____

_____

_____

_____

_____

What strategies can you employ to foster healthy, respectful disagreements that lead to more effective ideas?

_____

_____

_____

_____

_____

_____

Why is it important for leaders to periodically renovate existing systems within their organizations?

_____

_____

_____

_____

_____

_____

What qualities define "Level 5 Leaders" according to Jim Collins, and how can leaders embody these traits in their approach?

_____

_____

_____

_____

_____

How can you use your voice to bring about positive change and inspire others within their communities and organizations?

_____

_____

_____

_____

_____

_____

_____

What are two or three specific applications you want to make from this book?

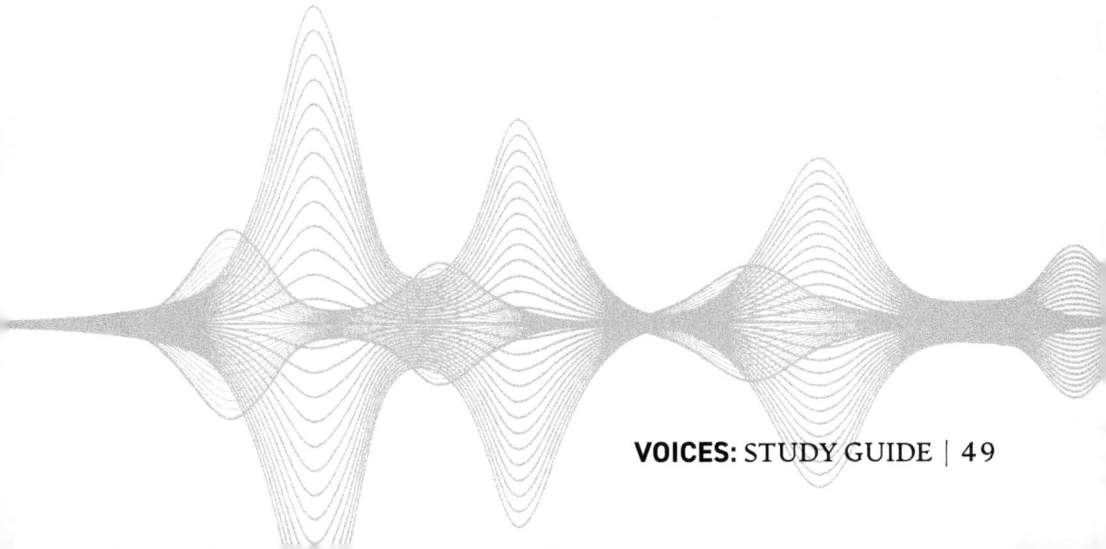

_____

_____

_____

_____

_____

_____

_____